BUSINESS BLOCKS WORKBOOK

TRANSFORM YOUR SELF-SABOTAGING MINDS GREMLINS, AWAKEN YOUR INNER MENTOR, AND ALLOW YOUR BUSINESS BRILLANCE TO SHINE

HOLLY WORTON

CONTENTS

A CIP catalogue record for this book is available from the British Library

First edition: 2016
Second edition: 2020

ISBN 978-1-911161-38-7

Published by Tribal Publishing Ltd

Please direct permissions requests to:
permissions@tribal-publishing.com

INTRODUCTION TO THE WORKBOOK

I truly hope that you enjoyed my book *Business Blocks: Transform Your Self-Sabotaging Mind Gremlins, Awaken Your Inner Mentor, and Allow Your Business Brilliance to Shine*. When I wrote the book, it was not meant to be a motivational self help book; it was meant to be a very experiential book.

In the interest of making it as easy as possible for you to take action on the topics I explored in *Business Blocks*, I've created this workbook. It contains the fifteen categories of business beliefs, questions to help you delve deeper so you can get clear on your current mindset and the mindset you want to have, and a list of journal prompts. Most importantly, it's got space for you to make your own notes and record your own observations about your experiences.

I hope you find this workbook to be useful!

1

HOW TO USE THIS WORKBOOK

> "My mother believed in curses, karma, good luck, bad luck, feng shui. Her amorphous set of beliefs showed me you can pick and choose the qualities of your philosophy, based on what works for you."
>
> Amy Tan

How you use this workbook is entirely up to you, and you alone will know the best way for you to work through the chapters based on what's right for you. You're the one who is actually going to do the work here. Be sure to tailor this to fit your own personal wants and needs.

You can use this workbook in a variety of ways:

- Read each chapter in order: do the work and answer the journal prompts that correspond to each chapter
- Dip in and out as you like
- Open the book at a random point and work on the chapter that you open up to
- Read through the table of contents and pick whichever chapter stands out to you

I do, however, suggest that you work on Chapter 2 first. That will help you to get clear on your big business vision so you know exactly what you want to be experiencing in your business and life. Then, the journal prompts in the individual categories will help you to delve even deeper into your mindset around each of the categories as they relate to your big vision.

And if you somehow came across this workbook without having read the original book, Business Blocks: Transform Your Self-Sabotaging Mind Gremlins, Awaken Your Inner Mentor, and Allow Your Business Brilliance to Shine, I'd recommend that you stop right now and get that book. It's available in ebook, paperback, and audiobook formats, and it's got vital information that will provide the foundation for the work you do in this workbook. This workbook is intended to support the original book and help you to go deeper. It's not intended as a stand-alone book.

Are you ready? Let's get started.

2

GET CLEAR ON WHAT YOU WANT

> "When you know what you want, and want it bad enough, you will find a way to get it."
>
> Jim Rohn

Before we get into the different categories of beliefs and the belief statements themselves, you need to know what you want. Are you 100% clear on the vision you have for your business and life? How do you want to step into your greatness and become a leader in your field? What do you want to experience in your business and life?

Back in 2015, I did a podcast episode on How to Get Clear on Your Big Business Vision (find it here: www.hollyworton.com/111/), which includes a guided meditation and a worksheet that walks you through each stage of this process to help you get clear on exactly what you want for your business. On that page, you can also find links to download both the meditation and also a pdf with these questions so that you can write them out.

I highly recommend that you print out this list or write the answers down in your journal (or get the workbook edition of this book, which has plenty of room to write down your answers). This is essential information that will help you to determine what you need to believe to make your dream a reality.

Visual

Let's imagine that you've fully stepped into your greatness and that you're living your big vision for your business and life.

What does stepping into your greatness mean to you?

What does that look like?

What do you see yourself doing?

How do you see yourself starting your day? What time do you get up? Do you set an alarm, or do you wake up naturally?

What does your morning ritual look like? How long does it last?

What do you eat/drink in the morning?

What do you do once your morning routine is over?

What time do you start working?

Do you work from home, or do you leave home to work? What does your office or workspace look like?

What do you work on? Your own creative projects? Do you do work for clients or with clients?

If you're working with clients, what does this look like? Envision yourself with one of these ideal clients.

Are you writing, creating art, or content for your business? Envision yourself doing whatever it is that you'll be doing once you've achieved this goal of your ideal business.

Take a look at your bank account. Either look at your bank statement, or access your account on your computer. Now that you've got your ideal business, how much money is in your checking/current account? And how much do you have in savings? How much do you have in investments and in your pension/retirement fund?

What does the rest of your day look like?

What do you eat/drink throughout the day?

What else do you do throughout the afternoon?

What time do you wrap up your work or creative activities?

What does your lifestyle look like? What else are you doing in your life, when you're not working directly on your business? What do you see yourself doing?

What do you see yourself doing for exercise/fitness? What time of the day do you exercise?

Where do you see yourself living? What country are you in? What city, town, or village? Is it an urban environment, or is it rural?

What does your home look like?

What does your evening or nighttime routine look like? How long does it last?

Is there anything else you need to look at to give you a clear vision of what things look like now you are living the life of your dreams? Take a few seconds to look at that.

As you reflect on your day, you see how your ideal day is different from your current lifestyle. What are some other things that are different?

Auditory

Once you've fully stepped into your greatness, what will you be saying to yourself? It could be: "I'm proud of myself," "I can't believe I did this," "I'm so happy that I made it," or something else.

What will you hear other people saying about you? It could be: "She's amazing," "Wow, I can't believe what she's done with her business," or something else.

What are your clients saying about you?

What else do you hear in your life, now that you've fully stepped into your greatness? What's going on in the background as you live your day? Do you hear children? Pets? Birds? Music? Other people?

Is your home in a quiet area, or is it bustling and active? What about your office or workplace?

Kinesthetic

How do you feel when you wake up in the morning?

How do you feel throughout the day? What are your energy levels like? What emotions are you feeling?

How do you feel in the evening as you're getting ready for bed?

Now that you've fully stepped into your greatness, how do you feel? Are you feeling free? Satisfied? Proud of yourself? Excited about the future? Write down all the things you feel.

What are you grateful for in your ideal lifestyle?

Dial it up

Often, our beliefs limit our vision for ourselves. Read through your answers and mark any details where you're playing small or hesitating to dream big. Dial up the intensity and the bigness of your vision: how can you make it better, more exciting, or more satisfying? No one else has to see this but you, so don't be afraid to make your dream bigger, better, and bolder.

As you dial up the intensity of this vision, pay attention to any fears or limiting beliefs that you have, and write those down. What fears do you have about living this ideal lifestyle? What will people think of you? Will you lose family or friends with this lifestyle change? What will they say about you? Do you believe you're worthy of having this dream? Are you deserving of living this life of your dreams? Write down all the "yes, buts".

Repeat

You can repeat this visualization or this process as many times as you like. You may want to repeat it every quarter, so you can get clarity on how your vision has grown and changed over the previous months. As we grow, our vision for our business changes and we need to understand precisely how our ideal business vision changes over time so we can adjust our goals, strategy, and business plan accordingly.

I've been talking a lot lately about stepping into your greatness, and when we're not in a good place, it can be hard to tap into our greatness and see what it is. So give yourself permission to dream big and to repeat this process regularly, so you can gradually step up your vision of what you want for your business and your life. Each time, you'll expand your vision of what's possible for your business and life.

Action plan

What are the top three actions you could take this week to bring you closer to stepping into your greatness?

Who do you need to be to take these actions?

What do you need to believe about yourself to take these actions easily?

What might stop you from taking these actions? What would you rather have instead? How would you rather feel about your action plan? What do you need to do/experience instead? What do you need to believe about yourself and your ability to complete this action plan?

Business beliefs

Who do you need to be to step into your greatness fully? Who do you need to be to achieve your big business vision?

What do you need to believe about yourself to step into your greatness fully?

What's stopping you from stepping into your greatness? What would you rather have instead? What do you need to do/experience instead?

Wrap it up

Is there anything else you need to add to the vision? Are there any specific goals that you need to add that you want to achieve as part of your vision for stepping into your greatness? Get it all out and into words that you can see. That will make it easier for you to identify specific beliefs in the lists that follow.

Take action today

If you haven't already, answer the questions that I've posed for you in this chapter. They'll help you dig up fears and limiting beliefs for you to work on. Then decide when you want to revisit these questions and put it in the calendar, so you remember to do it.

3

CATEGORIES OF BLOCKS

"The eye sees only what the mind is prepared to comprehend."

Robertson Davies

I've divided up these business blocks into the same fifteen categories I presented in my book Business Beliefs; I consider these to be the essential facets of business mindset that I've regularly worked on with clients over the years. The categories include:

1. Action and Goals
2. Change and Growth
3. Clients and Boundaries
4. Confidence and Self-Trust
5. Creativity
6. Leadership and Outsourcing
7. Learning
8. Lifestyle
9. Marketing and Sales
10. Money
11. Personal Power
12. Strategy, Clarity and Vision
13. Success and Opportunities
14. Value and Self-Worth
15. Visibility

You may find that you have more work to do in some areas, and you may find that you have very little work to do in other areas. In any case, it's worth going through each category and exploring the questions in each chapter. You may uncover blocks that you didn't even know you had.

I'm good at some things: for example, creativity and learning. Sometimes I'm good with action-taking and goal-setting. Sometimes I'm good with change and growth. I've struggled in the past with setting and upholding boundaries, but I've improved in that area. I've struggled throughout my life with self-confidence, self-trust, leadership, personal power, self-value, self-worth, and visibility. I've had to work hard to improve my marketing and sales practices, despite having over a decade of experience from my first company.

Some things I'm good at; others are a big challenge. I believe that it's essential for us to know our strengths as well as our weaknesses. Which of these fifteen areas of business blocks come naturally to you? Which ones are more difficult?

And as I've said multiple times, this is like peeling off the layers of the onion: there are some things that you won't be able to see in yourself today, but they'll become more apparent once you start doing the mindset work to release your blocks. If you want to make this process as efficient as possible, it's essential to be willing to dig deep and uncover the shadow stuff—including the things that make you very uncomfortable. But no matter how you do the work, things will get better. Even if you're only ready, willing, and able to work on the surface level blocks, you'll start to see results. As the quote at the beginning of this chapter says, you'll only be able to see the things today that you're ready to understand right now. With work, you'll be able to go deeper and deeper.

Action and Goals

Action-taking is a vital part of owning and operating a business. Let's go beyond that: it's an integral part of life. Without taking action, we won't get anywhere. Yet many of us procrastinate on taking the actions we need to take to achieve our goals in business and life. We're blocked in the area of action-taking and goal-setting.

Change and Growth

Being an entrepreneur means being able to embrace change and growth. When we're blocked in this area, we stay stuck and stagnant. We avoid innovation and development, and our business can quickly fail. Blocks in this area can be fatal to a business.

Clients and Boundaries

Customers and clients are the backbones of every business. Without them, the company won't exist. When we have blocks in this area, we obstruct the flow of money into our business and prevent any success.

Confidence and Self-Trust

When we lack self-confidence and self-trust, business feels painful. It seems impossible to achieve anything. We may feel inclined to give up before we even get started. Some people can fake it until they make it, but not everybody can do this. Others who have blocks in this area will stay stuck, paralyzed with fear.

Creativity

Being an entrepreneur is being creative: you're creating a business that you hope will be successful. And you'll be creating new products and services to offer to your customers and clients. When you're blocked in this area, it makes it hard to create new things, making your business boring and stagnant.

Leadership and Outsourcing

When you own a business, you're a leader, whether you like it or not. But do you have the belief in yourself to stand up and step into this leadership role? If not, your business will suffer. And if you can't effectively outsource tasks to employees or freelancers, you'll be overwhelmed and ineffective as a leader. It's important to release any blocks you may have in this area.

Learning

Being an entrepreneur means learning new things...constantly. It requires staying on top of industry trends. If you have blocks in this area because you believe you're not a fast learner, or you're not good with technology (for example), then your business will suffer.

Lifestyle

It's essential to create a business that fits into the lifestyle that you want. It makes no sense to leave a job you were unhappy with to build a company that makes you even more miserable. Your lifestyle is an integral part of your business, and if you have blocks about your ability to have the lifestyle that you want, then you'll end up with a company that you hate.

Marketing and Sales

Marketing and sales are how you get your customers and clients, the backbone of your business. If you've got blocks in this area, you won't be able to generate the revenue you need to grow your business. If the situation is truly dire, you may end up with a costly hobby instead of a business. You wouldn't be the first.

Money

Money: if it's not flowing into your business, then something's not right. Many people have such severe money blocks that it affects their ability to create and grow a business. That's why this is one of the essential categories of business blocks.

Personal Power

Personal power is a feeling—a sense of being—made up of the layers of self-trust, self-love, self-acceptance, self-esteem, self-confidence, self-value, self-worth that we have within ourselves. It's a sense of groundedness. And if we have blocks in this area, it will make it very, very difficult to create a successful business. We need to trust ourselves, love ourselves, accept ourselves, value ourselves and have confidence in ourselves. This work is a big project that can take years to achieve, and the sooner we get started, the sooner we'll see results.

Strategy, Clarity, and Vision

Running a successful business is all about having a clear vision (see chapter 7) and a plan to achieve it. Some people are so blocked that they don't know what they want for their business, much less understand how they're going to get there. So they take random actions, wandering around in circles. If you're blocked in this area, you may feel like you've been taking shots in the dark and not hitting anything—because you don't even know what you're aiming at.

Success and Opportunities

Success means different things to different people. Having a successful business may be about making seven figures each year. It may mean bringing in just enough money but having the flexibility to have a rewarding family life. If we're blocked in this area—either because we're afraid of failure, or we're scared of success, or something else entirely—it's going to make it very, very difficult to build the business we want.

Value and Self-Worth

When we don't value ourselves, we find it hard to succeed. We find it challenging to get clients, and when we do, we may undercharge and overdeliver. It's hard to run a business this way, and when we have self-worth blocks, this can often lead to a company never getting off the ground.

Visibility

If people don't know who you are, then they can't hire you or buy your products. If you're the best-kept secret in your field, then you won't be bringing in business. Visibility blocks can cost you your success. If you're afraid of standing out in the crowd, then it's pretty much guaranteed that you're going to blend in—and that's not good for business.

4

ACTION AND GOAL BLOCKS

"Any action is often better than no action, especially if you have been stuck in an unhappy situation for a long time. If it is a mistake, at least you learn something, in which case it's no longer a mistake. If you remain stuck, you learn nothing."

Eckhart Tolle

Discover your blocks

Here are a few questions to help you get clear on your business blocks:

Let's look at your business goals. Have you set clear goals that are specific and measurable? Are they written down where you can review them regularly?

Do you review your goals periodically?

Do you have a clear plan to achieve these goals? If not, what's stopping you? What are you afraid of?

What beliefs do you hold that are preventing you from setting clear goals and creating a plan to achieve them?

One of the best ways to uncover blocks in this area is to ask yourself the following question: what do you procrastinate on? Often the things we most procrastinate on are the things that take us out of our comfort zone. Interestingly, these are also actions that will lead us to more significant results in our business. So...what are you procrastinating on? And why?

What's stopping you from prioritizing your to-do list and getting started?

And what's stopping you from choosing three of the most critical tasks on your to-do list each day and getting those done first?

What's stopping you from selecting ten of the little things on your list and outsourcing them to a virtual assistant? For this exercise, don't use money as a reason: assume you've got the funds to hire a VA and then ask yourself the question: why haven't you hired one yet?

Do you struggle to delegate tasks to someone else because you're afraid they won't get completed to your standards?

Are you a perfectionist? Is that why things aren't getting done on your list?

Do you struggle to live by the motto "good enough is better than perfect"?

Why do you think you find it so challenging to create content regularly, like blog posts, email newsletters, or podcast episodes (assuming this is part of your business strategy)?

What's holding you back from batching and releasing content consistently?

What might make it easier for you?

Are you afraid of taking up space on people's Facebook timelines? Do you worry about "bothering" people with your content?

What's holding you back from creating a structured signature system or online program (again, assuming this is part of your business strategy)? Is this something you want to do, or do you think you should do it because "everyone else is"?

Do you believe that there's no natural system for what you do?

Are you afraid of standing out and being judged for creating your system?

Discover your fears

What fears do you have around actions and goals?

Are you afraid of taking the wrong actions?

Are you afraid of making decisions?

Are you afraid of doing a lot of work and still failing?

Are you afraid of not achieving goals?

Are you afraid of achieving a goal and realizing it's not what we really wanted?

What else are you afraid of?

5

CHANGE AND GROWTH BLOCKS

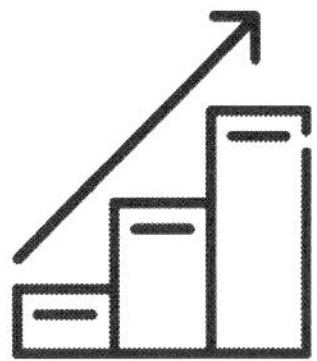

"Change will not come if we wait for some other person or some other time. We are the ones we've been waiting for. We are the change that we seek."
Barack Obama

Discover your blocks

Here are a few questions to help you get clear on your business blocks:

Why do you think your business is exactly the same today as it was six months ago?

Why is your income still the same?

Why are you still frustrated with the same things?

What's stopping you from changing things up and bringing in more clients?

Why do you think you haven't you gotten help with the things that frustrate you and make you feel stuck in your business?

What's holding you back from re-branding your business or even changing your niche? Is it because everyone knows you as the [insert your business niche here] expert?

Do you believe that if you change your brand or your niche, people will think you're unprofessional? Are you afraid of looking like you're "too big for your britches"? That people might judge you for expanding into a new look for your business?

Why haven't you quit your job yet, assuming it's the right moment to dedicate yourself full time to your business? Is it because you're afraid to take the leap of faith in your business and let go of the steady pay check? Is it because you don't believe, deep down, that you have what it takes to run a successful business?

Are you afraid that your recent success is all a fluke, and it's all going to go downhill sometime soon?

Why haven't you made plans to find another business coach or mentor? Is it because you're afraid that your new coach night not be as good as this one is? Are you afraid of hurting your current mentor's feelings by making a change?

What's stopping you from hiring a virtual assistant? Is it because you're wondering how you can possibly outsource these tasks to someone else?

Are you stressing that they won't get done exactly how you do them?

Are you worried that your VA will do things differently (meaning: not as good as you)? Are you thinking that it's better to keep doing these tasks yourself...that way you have full control over how things get done?

Discover your fears

What fears do you have around change and growth?

Are you afraid of change?

Are you afraid of not being able to change and staying the same forever?

Are you afraid of the unknown?

Are you afraid of outgrowing a group of business friends?

Are you afraid of not being able to handle the things that come with change?

What else are you afraid of?

6

CLIENTS AND BOUNDARY BLOCKS

"When you're the most successful person in your family, in your neighborhood, and in your town, everybody thinks you're the First National Bank, and you have to figure out for yourself where those boundaries are."

Oprah Winfrey

Discover your blocks

Here are a few questions to help you get clear on your business blocks:

What's stopping you from having a steady stream of clients? Are you charging by the hour for individual sessions, rather than creating packages that your ideal clients would find attractive?

Are you afraid of asking clients for the more substantial sum of money that a package would cost because it just seems cheaper and more accessible for them to work with you by the hour?

Why is it that you think you need to be available 24 hours a day, seven days a week for your clients? Do you believe that if you're not always there for them, then they'll work with someone else?

Are you afraid that if you don't go overtime with your sessions, that your clients won't feel like they've had great value from your work together?

Do you believe that "nice coaches/therapists/whatever" give their clients extra time for free?

Why do you think you struggle to attract great clients?

Are you clear on who your ideal clients are, and why you love them so much?

Do you find it hard to say no to clients who express interest in working with you?

Is it difficult to refer potential clients to someone else if they don't feel like a good fit? Do you believe you have to take on every client that comes your way?

Are you so desperate for the money that you feel like you have to take every client who approaches you?

Why do you think you're attracting people who like what you do but aren't willing to invest?

Could you change the way you market your business and try to attract clients who are willing to pay your fees?

Do you truly understand the value of the work that you do with clients, or do you secretly believe that your work isn't good enough? (If this is the case, refer to the chapter on Value and Self-Worth Blocks, which will help you dig even deeper into this area.)

What's stopping you from getting testimonials from all of your clients?

Are you afraid that they'll say no?

Are you worried they'll tell you they didn't get any results from the work that they did with you, and that it was a waste of money?

Are you worried that you'll annoy them by asking for a testimonial?

Discover your fears

What fears do you have around clients and boundaries?

Are you afraid that you'll never have enough clients?

Are you afraid that clients will never pay what you want to earn?

Are you afraid that clients will hate the way you work?

Are you afraid that clients will be upset when you cancel a session because they were late?

Are you afraid of bad reviews online?

What else are you afraid of?

7

LIFESTYLE BLOCKS

"Go confidently in the direction of your dreams! Live the life you've imagined."

Henry David Thoreau

Discover your blocks

Here are a few questions to help you get clear on your business blocks:

Is your team working effectively and efficiently?

Perhaps you need to restructure things?

Are you afraid of letting go of more aspects of your business to your staff?

What's stopping you from taking a look at that admin that "only you can do" and see if someone else can take it over?

What's the worst that would happen if you stopped working evenings and weekends?

What makes you think that you can't achieve the exciting lifestyle you dream of?

What do other online entrepreneurs have that you don't?

What are they like that you're not like?

Are they doing something that you aren't doing?

Is it possible that you believe you don't deserve that kind of lifestyle?

What's stopping you from only taking on clients for Zoom, Skype, or telephone sessions?

Are you afraid you'll lose them all?

Do you worry that no one will want to see you for Skype sessions?

Have you ever even tried telling potential clients that you only do remote sessions?

What's the worst that could happen if you just drew the line and began offering only remote sessions?

What's going on with the lack of upgrades in your lifestyle?

Have you been investing all your business profits, or have you been spending the money on other things?

What would it feel like to make a list of the top three things you'd really like to upgrade in your life and then actually make it happen?

Do you have any beliefs about it being impossible to have a successful business and the perfect partner?

Do you believe you can only have one or the other?

What's stopping you from going out there and meeting the right person for you?

What's keeping you from at least going out to places where you might meet someone?

Discover your fears

What fears do you have around lifestyle?

Are you afraid that you can't have it all?

Are you afraid that you need to work so hard you'll never have time to relax?

Are you afraid that family will leave you because you're working too hard?

Are you afraid that you'll never be able to slow down?

Are you afraid of never having the life you want?

What else are you afraid of?

8

MARKETING AND SALES BLOCKS

"The aim of marketing is to know and understand the customer so well the product or service fits him and sells itself."

Peter Drucker

Discover your blocks

Here are a few questions to help you get clear on your business blocks:

What's stopping you from attending business networking events?

Have you tried different types of groups, or did you attend one and decide to call it quits?

What's going on with the elevator pitch for you?

Do you hate going around in a circle and hearing everyone's minute, or are you terrified of standing up and speaking about yourself?

What's going on for you with the more informal, conversational networking?

Do you struggle to talk about your business coherently?

Are you afraid of how you come across?

What's stopping you from really stepping up your marketing in a big way: doing joint ventures and running Facebook ads to build your community so you can run events?

Have you tried asking your current email list if they're interested in workshops and retreats?

Have you put this idea out there at all in any way?

What's stopping you? Are you afraid people won't be interested?

What is it that scares you about speaking?

What's preventing you from joining Toastmasters or some other organization that might help you to be a good speaker?

Why do you think you're feeling insecure about your message?

What's the worst that could happen if you spoke to a group, and they weren't very receptive?

Do you have any icky memories from the past when you made a big mistake in a school presentation, and everyone laughed at you?

What's stopping you from offering discovery sessions to potential clients? They can be a good way of getting to know someone and allowing them to get to know you and see if you're a good fit.

Do you believe that all sales conversations are sleazy?

Do you think that it's impossible to be congruent when selling to a potential client?

How are you afraid of coming across in a sales conversation?

Would it feel any different if you were to view them as an invitation for people to work with you?

Would it be different if you just saw them as a way to connect with people, with no attachment to the outcome of getting a new client?

What's going on for you with webinars?

Is it fear of technology and speaking, or is it something else?

What's the worst that could happen if a webinar went wrong? And what does "going wrong" mean to you?

What do you envision in your webinar nightmares?

Do you believe that they're just not for you?

Discover your fears

What fears do you have around marketing and sales?

Are you afraid of public speaking?

Are you afraid of people thinking you're pushy if you sell to them?

Are you afraid that no one will want what you have to offer?

Are you afraid of taking up too much space in people's social media timelines?

Are you afraid of people unsubscribing from your newsletter?

What else are you afraid of?

9

MONEY BLOCKS

"When we do what we are meant to do, money comes to us, doors open for us, we feel useful, and the work we do feels like play to us."

Julia Cameron

Discover your blocks

Here are a few questions to help you get clear on your business blocks:

What's stopping you from generating more than just the bare minimum?

Do you have any limiting beliefs around making MORE than enough money?

What's happening with your lack of savings?

Are you afraid that if you start to save money, you'll lose it somehow?

Do you believe that you don't deserve to live a comfortable life with savings?

What's going on with all the expenses?

Do you feel like you have to spend as much as you earn?

Is there anything you could cut back on? (What does that question bring up for you?)

When you look in your bank account and see money in there, do you believe you have to spend every last penny, just because you have it?

Do you think that you've got some business curse on you and that you'll never create a successful business?

Are you not worthy of having a company that brings in money?

Do you think you don't know how to build a thriving business?

What's stopping you from letting go of your past companies that didn't make it?

What's the worst that could happen if this business became wildly successful beyond your imagination?

What's making you think so negatively about your business?

Do you have a plan to create sufficient income to pay off your debt?

What's stopping you from focusing on bringing in money, rather than your fear of debt?

Do you feel like it's not right for you to make money when it's so easy for you to do what you do?

That somehow you're not deserving of receiving lots of money for your work?

Or do you have issues around you not worthy of making lots of money... easily?

Discover your fears

What fears do you have around money?

Are you afraid that you'll never have enough?

Are you afraid that you'll go bankrupt?

Are you afraid that you'll earn so much that people will ask you for loans?

Are you afraid that you'll earn so much money that your friends will think you're a snob?

Are you afraid that making too much money will turn you into a bad person?

What else are you afraid of?

10

PERSONAL POWER BLOCKS

"Personal power... is made up of the layers of self-trust, self-love, self-acceptance, self-esteem, self-confidence, self-value, self-worth."

The Grandmothers, If Trees Could Talk

Discover your blocks

Here are a few questions to help you get clear on your business blocks:

Why don't you believe you can make a difference in the world?

Do you think that you make a difference in your clients' lives?

What's stopping you from stepping up into a role where you can help people on a much bigger scale?

What's stopping you from accepting your part in making the world a better place just as you are today?

What's the worst that could happen if you tried to make a positive difference in the world?

What makes you think you can't grow to the size of those prominent online business personalities?

What's stopping you from growing into that role?

What's holding you back from just being yourself and shining your light even brighter?

Are you afraid of being more visible in the world?

What gives you the idea that you don't have what it takes to achieve your big business vision?

Who do you think you need to be to achieve this vision?

What's stopping you from achieving this vision?

What makes you feel powerless to achieve your goals?

What makes it hard to focus on your business, rather than being swayed by all that you read online?

What's stopping you from cutting out the noise and just focusing on your business and what you know you want to do?

Do you believe you're not strong enough to stand your ground and build your business based on your wants and interests?

What is it about the word "powerful" that sounds dirty?

And why do you think only bad people are powerful?

Can you think of any examples of influential people who did excellent work in the world, and who made a positive difference?

What do you think is stopping you from feeling powerful?

What do you need to believe about yourself to feel powerful in a good way?

Discover your fears

What fears do you have around personal power?

Are you afraid of being seen as a tyrant?

Are you afraid of being attacked for your beliefs?

Are you afraid that people won't like you if you stand up for what you believe in?

Are you afraid that being a strong person will be a turnoff to people?

Are you afraid of being different?

What else are you afraid of?

11

STRATEGY, CLARITY AND VISION BLOCKS

"At the end of the day, when it comes time to make that decision ... all you have to guide you are your values, and your vision, and the life experiences that make you who you are."

Michelle Obama

Discover your blocks

Here are a few questions to help you get clear on your business blocks:

What's keeping you stuck?

What is it about your previous business plans that no longer feel right?

What would feel right for your business?

Do you have any beliefs around not being able to choose a clear path for your business?

Are there any beliefs around trusting your decisions? (Also, have you worked with a business coach or mentor lately?

The right coach/mentor could help you out of this situation once you've cleared up any limiting beliefs or blocks around strategy, clarity, and vision. This concept applies to the other points here, too.)

What's stopping you from choosing something and trying it out?

Do you have any fears around failure if it doesn't work out?

Are there any beliefs about being good enough at something to charge for it?

Are you afraid that you don't know how to create a clear vision for a business?

What's stopping you from upgrading your activities from hobby to business?

What's holding you back from taking this out into the world in a more significant way?

What would your dream business look like?

What's stopping you from dreaming bigger?

Are there any fears around giving up a steady paycheck?

Why do you think you struggle to create a clear vision that would transform your hobby into a business?

What do you need to believe about yourself to turn this hobby into a business?

What do you think is going on behind this trial and error approach to your company?

What's stopping you from selecting a clear business model and trying it out?

What's preventing you from hiring a coach or mentor to help you with this?

Do you have any doubts about your ability to apply a clear strategy to your business?

What do you think is stopping you from taking your business global?

Do you have any fears around opening up and sharing your business with the world?

Are there any fears around your ability to attract a wider audience?

Do you struggle to dream bigger with your business?

Does anything about having an online business scare you?

Discover your fears

What fears do you have around strategy, clarity, and vision?

Are you afraid of picking the wrong strategy?

Are you afraid that you'll never be able to see a clear path forward in your business?

Are you afraid of picking the wrong business model?

Are you afraid that you'll never know what to do?

Are you afraid of focusing on the wrong income streams?

What else are you afraid of?

12

SUCCESS AND OPPORTUNITY BLOCKS

"Success is peace of mind which is a direct result of self-satisfaction in knowing you did your best to become the best you are capable of becoming."

John Wooden

Discover your blocks

Here are a few questions to help you get clear on your business blocks:

Why do you think you're feeling stuck and frustrated in your business?

What's going on that you're not happy with?

Do you ever feel like everyone else is successful in business, and you aren't?

Do you ever feel like you're afraid of success?

What's the worst that could happen if you were wildly successful beyond your dreams?

What have you been doing to create success in your business, and what things have you been avoiding doing?

Are any fears or limiting beliefs preventing you from taking action towards your goals so that you can create business success?

How do you define business success? It's different for everyone, and if you see another entrepreneur living a spectacularly successful life, think about what's stopping you from adding some of the things she has to your list of goals and then taking action towards those goals?

Have you stayed in touch with Big Name Coach and her community since doing her mentoring program?

What's stopping you from getting back in touch and letting her know you love what she's doing now, and you'd like to be involved if she feels like it's a good fit?

Do you have any fears or blocks around approaching her? Might you be afraid of being rejected?

How often do you keep in touch with your coaching school and its founders?

Are they aware that you'd love to participate more? What might prevent you from staying in touch more, or reconnecting and letting them know that you're available for speaking? On a practical level, do you have a Speaking page on your website so that everyone knows you're available as a speaker?

How does the idea of creating one make you feel? Are there any blocks there?

Does that trigger any fears of visibility or rejection?

Discover your fears

What fears do you have around success and opportunities?

Are you afraid of failure?

Are you afraid of success?

Are you afraid of not seeing opportunities when they come to you?

Are you afraid of picking the wrong opportunities?

Are you afraid of being more successful than your peers?

What else are you afraid of?

13

VALUE AND SELF-WORTH BLOCKS

"Over the years, I've interviewed thousands of people, most of them women, and I would say that the root of every dysfunction I've ever encountered, every problem, has been some sense of a lacking of self-value or of self-worth."

Oprah Winfrey

Discover your blocks

Here are a few questions to help you get clear on your business blocks:

What's holding you back from offering your new coaching program to the people in your community?

Do you feel that it's not good enough? Too expensive? Do you worry that no one would sign up for it?

Do you believe that your clients don't want a big package?

What's the worst that could happen if you picked your five favorite clients and offered them this new package?

What's going on with your testimonials?

Are you afraid that people might give you negative feedback rather than glowing praise?

Are you worried that you'll bother people if you ask them for help? That they won't want to make it known that they've worked with you?

What's stopping you from asking for testimonials?

Does putting up praise on your website feel snobbish? (Think: "Look at me! I'm so good.")

Why do you think it's essential for you to compare your rates to those of other people in your field?

What do you think is keeping you at the low end of the pricing spectrum?

Are you staying cheap on purpose?

Do you feel like you aren't good enough to charge more?

That you aren't worth more?

What's the worst that could happen if you raised your rates?

What's making you overwhelm your clients with such a robust offering?

Are you aware that you might be suffering from Kitchen Sink Syndrome, where you throw in everything but the kitchen sink in an attempt to make sure that your clients get more than they expected?

Does this mean that you value your core offerings so little that you have to add more, more, more?

How do you feel about the value of your basic online program? Is it enough? If not, why?

What's holding you back from actually offering paid services to people?

If someone from networking (or elsewhere) has expressed interest in what you do, how does it feel to imagine quoting your prices to them?

What beliefs do you have around receiving money for your expertise?

Do you think you're worth it?

Discover your fears

What fears do you have around value and self-worth?

Are you afraid of not being good enough?

Are you afraid of not being worthy of success?

Are you afraid of not knowing enough?

Are you afraid of not being smart enough?

Are you afraid that you're not ready?

What else are you afraid of?

14

VISIBILITY BLOCKS

"Cultivate visibility because attention is currency."
Chris Brogan

Discover your blocks

Here are a few questions to help you get clear on your business blocks:

What's stopping you from setting up those Facebook ads?

What's the worst that could happen if unknown people saw them?

Are you afraid of getting negative comments? Haters? People saying bad things about you?

What kinds of negative things are you scared of people saying?

What's the worst thing that someone could say about you?

What's wrong with how you look and sound on video?

What kind of offensive comments are you imagining?

Are you afraid that people will dislike what you have to say in your videos?

That they'll think what you have to say isn't valid?

Are you scared that people will laugh at you?

What do you need to believe about yourself to make it easier to create and publish videos on YouTube and Facebook?

What's so scary about Facebook groups?

What does this trigger for you?

What's stopping you from speaking up and participating?

What do you think people will say or think about you?

Are you afraid of posting something inappropriate?

What's the worst that could happen?

What's stopping you from promoting your blog posts to a broader audience?

Are you afraid that people will think you don't know what you're talking about? That your message is too basic? That you're not good enough?

What's going on with your webinars?

Are you afraid that people will attend your online trainings and think you're a fraud? That they'll call you out on how little you know? That you'll be caught without an answer? That they'll say that you don't know enough to run a business around what you do?

What's the worst that could happen if you ran a webinar and opened yourself up to people's feedback?

Discover your fears

What fears do you have around visibility?

Are you afraid of standing out in the crowd?

Are you afraid of being seen?

Are you afraid of getting too much attention?

Are you afraid of criticism and negative comments?

Are you afraid of expressing yourself fully?

What else are you afraid of?

APPENDIX I

TRANSFORM YOUR BUSINESS BLOCKS INTO BUSINESS BLISS

"Personal transformation can and does have global effects. As we go, so goes the world, for the world is us. The revolution that will save the world is ultimately a personal one."

Marianne Williamson

The first step is to become aware of your business blocks, and the power of doing the work to uncover them is that now you've got the clarity you need to transform them into business strengths. How? By releasing your blocks at the subconscious level.

Remember when I talked about how powerful the subconscious mind was at the beginning of this book? Well, now we need to harness the power of the subconscious mind so we can release these fears and blocks at that profound level.

You could do this by working with a practitioner or therapist or by doing the work with yourself. I recommend a combination of the two. I regularly use a process called PSYCH-K® with myself to transform my business mindset, but I also work with another PSYCH-K® facilitator to help me uncover my blocks and get to the core of what's going on for me. And whenever I have a session with my coach/mentor Lisa Wechtenhiser, that also brings up loads of stuff for me to work on.

As I've said before, it's vital that you find the process or technique that works best for you. That's why I haven't included a specific process in this book: what works for me may or may not work for you. And besides, even if I were to teach you a process like Heart-centered Energy Work®, that would be a whole book in itself. The process that works for you could be PSYCH-K®, or it could be NLP, EFT, TAT, hypnotherapy, or something else. You might need to try a few different techniques before you find what works for you. I include PSYCH-K® as an example in many of my stories because that's what works for me.

I hope you've found this book to be useful. I've tried to keep it short and simple, so you can quickly and easily identify the blocks that are keeping you stuck in your business. Awareness is the first step, and releasing your fears and blocks at the subconscious is super essential if you want to upgrade your business mindset.

Think about the following: what does it cost you to avoid doing this deep mindset work? It's so easy to put off and just keep doing what you've been doing. But what will your business be like six months from now if you don't take action? If you don't get clarity on the mindset shifts that you need to make? If you don't make those changes?

It's time to let those mind gremlins out of their cage, where they're trapped in your subconscious mind.

Take action today

Are you wondering what you need to do now? I've broken it all down into five easy action steps. We've got to take action and put the time in. Transforming our mindset doesn't need to be difficult, but it isn't exactly magic. It does require an investment of time and action.

Here's how to get started:

1. Identify the core blocks that you need to shift in your business mindset, using the methods and questions described in this book. Get my first book, Business Beliefs: Upgrade Your Mindset to Overcome Self-Sabotage, Achieve Your Goals, and Transform Your Business (and Life), and work through that book to get even more clarity.
2. Find the best technique for you to change your mindset at the subconscious level.
3. Find the best practitioner or facilitator to help you with this mindset transformation, and/or do the work yourself.
4. Do the inner work to transform your mindset.
5. Take action to reinforce your new mindset.
6. Repeat.

1. Identify the blocks you need to shift

Identify the fears and blocks that you need to change in your business mindset, using the methods described in this book. Spend time journaling to get clear on what you do want to experience, and which blocks you need to release in order to make that happen.

2 and 3. Find the best process and practitioner

This may involve trial and error. If something doesn't feel quite right, then don't go back again. You don't owe them anything. Listen to your gut feeling on this, and if you don't see changes reasonably soon, you might want to reevaluate whether you've found the best method (or practitioner) for you.

After hearing so many great things about PSYCH-K®, I was tremendously disappointed in the first facilitator I saw. It was a terrible session, and I never went back to see her again. I then sought out another facilitator, but she convinced me to try ThetaHealing® instead, which I did enjoy, but I still wasn't working with the process that I wanted to try. Finally, I found a facilitator I liked and had an excellent session with her. A week or so later, I trained in the PSYCH-K® Basic Workshop.

There are many processes and techniques out there, and there are many facilitators and practitioners of each one. Sometimes it can be tricky to find what's right for you. It can take trial and error. That's why I haven't included a specific process in this book: what works for me may or may not work for you. And besides, even if I were to teach you a process like Heart-centered Energy Work®, that would be a whole book in itself.

Some of the processes and techniques you might like to try include:

- Heart-centered Energy Work®
- PSYCH-K®
- ThetaHealing®
- Emotional Freedom Techniques® (EFT or tapping)
- NLP (Neuro-Linguistic Programming)
- TAT (Tapas Acupressure Technique)
- Ask & Receive
- hypnotherapy
- ...and more

I've also experienced sound therapy sessions and light language sessions. In 2019, I graduated from a Shamanic Plant Spirit Healing Apprenticeship, which does what it says in the name: it taught me how to work with plant spirits for healing (which, of course, can also help to free ourselves from our blocks).

Change can be rapid when you're working at the subconscious and energetic levels, so there's no need to attend weekly sessions for months before seeing results. Stay alert, and pay attention to how your life and business are different since you started doing the mindset work. Sometimes significant changes occur, but people don't notice because things are going well, and they're no longer experiencing whatever it was that they wanted to let go of. That's why it's so useful to write things down in a journal.

4. Do the training yourself

I always recommend that people train in a process or technique themselves so they can do the work on their own. There is great power in being able to release your blocks whenever you want, wherever you want, however you want. I have spent the past several years working on my blocks regularly (at least once a week!), and I also see other professionals from time to time. In my experience, this is the perfect combination to approach releasing our business blocks.

If you've found a process that you particularly like, train in it and learn how to do it for yourself. This will require an initial investment, but it will save you time and money in the long run. You'll be able to make significant changes in your belief system, and you'll be reaping the results in your business. This process is what I mean when I say "do the inner work."

5. Take inspired action

When I work with clients, I always help them create a short action plan at the end of each session. This is important: no matter how much work we do to release our blocks and transform our mindset, we also have to take practical action. We can release as many blocks as we want, but if we don't do the work in our business, we won't automatically create change.

We still need to write the blog posts, do the videos, market our business online, and make the sales calls.

I always say this is like climbing a spiral staircase: the left step is the mindset work; the right step is the practical action. Left, right, left, right, and up we go as we build our business.

Next, I talk a little bit about how you can work with others if you feel drawn to do so. If not, I encourage you to read through the chapter, so you can at least have some point of comparison to other professionals that you may choose to work with. It helps to have an idea of how different people work so you can find what's best for you.

Remember: you know what's best for you! There's a reason I keep saying this: we can have the tendency to give our power away to others, but deep down, you're the one who knows what's best. Go with your gut feeling or with whatever your heart says. That's your higher self checking in with you to let you know which option is best.

APPENDIX II

NEED MORE HELP?

> "Whether it's your family, friends, community that you connect with, don't be afraid to reach out. That's my biggest advice that I can say for anyone going through any kind of obstacle or trials or tribulations. Don't be afraid to reach out and ask questions. Ask for help, because you never know where you'll find it."
>
> Vanessa Williams

Are you feeling stuck? If you've read this book, and are still feeling like you need more help engaging the power of your inner wisdom, read on. Or perhaps you've taken the five inspired action steps, and you uncovered some fears, blocks, or limiting beliefs that have gotten in the way of you honing your business intuition. If that's the case, get help.

Is this you?

Are you a coach, a healer, or a holistic therapist? Maybe you've got another type of business, and you're on a mission to change the world through the work that you do. You may be just starting in business, or you may be in the process of growing your existing business.

But you've hit a rough spot. You've done all the business and marketing training, but somehow things just aren't flowing for you. You're feeling stuck and frustrated.

All you want is more clients so you can help more people (and, let's face it, make a decent living from your business). You're starting to realize that being successful in business isn't just about knowing how to market and run a business. It's also about your mindset: making sure that your beliefs and your inner dialogue are aligned with your vision and goals.

But it's not always that easy.

Maybe you're struggling with:

- Lack of confidence, which leads to you procrastinating on getting your Most Important Tasks completed.
- Fear that people won't get what you do. They won't want it, or else they won't be willing to pay you for it.
- Issues around visibility and fear of standing out in the online crowd.
- Fear of overwhelm if you do attract all the clients you want and build a thriving business.
- Getting started with social media marketing, speaking, videos, and webinars—the thought of any of this makes you cringe.
- Believing you have something precious to offer. I mean, you know you do, but—do you?

Have you ever experienced any of this?

If so, you're not alone. I struggled with this stuff when I started my second business, and until I found a solution to all of this, my business suffered.

Fortunately, I found an easy solution to all of this. One that's fast, effective, and painless. It transformed my business, and it changed my life.

Imagine how it would feel if:

- You only attracted great clients: people who know what they want and they value what you do.
- You felt nourished and fulfilled by your business, confident that you were making a difference in the world, client by client.
- You had a tribe of raving fans who were eager to sign up for your new product or service launches.
- You had a clear vision for your business that felt aligned with your purpose: 100% you.
- Your business felt like it was in flow, with a regular stream of clients ready to invest in what you have to offer.

Sound good?

This scenario is what I want for you. I want to help purpose-driven women entrepreneurs create the business of their dreams that allows them to live the lifestyle they want.

As I mentioned earlier in the book, I've stepped back from doing one-to-one sessions so I can focus on my writing. However, I do offer occasional sessions, as well as done-for-you mindset and energy work, in my Patreon community.

Head over to www.patreon.com/hollyworton and check it out. Please get in touch if you have any questions: holly@hollyworton.com.

Podcast

As you've seen at the end of some chapters, I've got many podcast episodes on mindset. These episodes are a great way to deepen your understanding of your mindset and find new ways of transforming your business beliefs. Most podcast episodes have full transcripts available on the website, either to read directly or as a free pdf download (no email required).

One-to-one work

If you're ready to get started with one-to-one sessions right now, I have some recommendations for you. These are five women that I trust entirely and often go to for sessions myself. They all work online via Skype/Zoom.

I highly recommend these five facilitators:

- Cara Wilde: http://carawilde.com
- Cazzie Dare: https://yearning4learning.co.uk/
- Claire Baker: http://happyhealthyempowered.com/
- Jo Trewartha: http://freeyourmindsolutions.com/
- Sharon Lock: http://sharonlock.com

Take Action Today

1. Check out my Patreon and see if you're interested in how I can help you there.
2. Subscribe to my podcast (Into the Woods with Holly Worton) and listen to the episodes on mindset.
3. Find a process or technique that resonates with you and a facilitator to have sessions with.
4. Once you find a technique that you love, train in it so you can use it to work with yourself.
5. If you want to do a deep dive into your business beliefs, buy the Business Blocks workbook.

APPENDIX III

ON THE PODCAST

The Into the Woods podcast is all about going into the woods of you. I've got plenty of episodes that discuss all areas of mindset and business beliefs. This is a great way to deepen your understanding of your own mindset, and find new ways of transforming your business beliefs. Most podcast episodes have full transcripts available on the website, either to read directly or as a free pdf download (no email required).

You can find the full list of podcast episodes here:
www.hollyworton.com/podcast

How to get clear on what you want

- 195 Holly Worton ~ How to Stay Grounded + Strong in Your Vision
- 111 Holly Worton ~ How to Get Clear on Your Big Business Vision

Action and Goals

- 181 Jo + Holly ~ Is Mindset Important in Business, or Is It Just an Excuse to Avoid Action?
- 166 Holly Worton ~ How to Drop the Hustle and Start Taking Easy Inspired Action Instead

Change and Growth

- 333 Holly Worton ~ Do You Have a Fixed Mindset or a Growth Mindset?
- 332 Joanna Hennon + Holly ~ How to Step Into a New Identity Even When You're Not Sure What It Looks Like
- 273 Holly Worton ~ What Change Actually Looks Like
- 251 Holly Worton ~ How to Step Into a New Business Identity
- 196 Marianne Cantwell ~ How to Make Big Changes in Your Business in an Unconventional Way
- 64 How to Tame Your Business Beast and Automate Your Growth, with Tina Forsyth

Clients and Boundaries

- 184 Rebecca Miller ~ How to Use Case Studies to Get Great Publicity & Reach Your Ideal Clients
- 173 Jo & Holly ~ Should You Guarantee Results For Your Clients
- 154 Arabelle Yee ~ How to Create Unique Packages Personalized for Each Client
- 143 RM Harrison ~ How to Clone Your Favorite Client
- 121 Jo Casey ~ How to Get Coaching Clients Without the Hustle
- 106 Nicci Bonfanti ~ How to Serve Your Clients Through Selling
- 82 How to Create a High End Offer Your Clients Will Buy, with Julia Bernard-Thompson
- 38 How to Get More Clients Saying Yes, with Catherine Watkin

Confidence and Self-Trust

- 285 Holly Worton ~ How to Trust in Yourself & Trust That Everything is Working Out
- 243 Holly Worton ~ How to Trust Yourself in Business
- 213 Holly Worton ~ How to Face the Shadow Side of Visibility With Confidence
- 78 How to Get Confidence & Crush Self-Doubt, with Jenn Scalia

Creativity

- 291 Holly Worton ~ How to Open Up & Be Vulnerable in Your Creative Ventures
- 249 Holly Worton ~ How to Help Your Business Blossom in Creative New Ways
- 83 How to Follow Your Creative Intuition, with Flora Bowley

Leadership and Outsourcing

- 247 Holly Worton ~ What, When, Why, and How to Outsource

Sales and Marketing

- 255 Jo Casey + Holly ~ How to Navigate the New Era of Email Marketing
- 228 Holly Worton ~ How to Be Consistent in Marketing Your Business (And Why It's So Important)
- 218 Stella Orange ~ How to Experiment With New Ways of Marketing That Don't Feel Manipulative
- 212 Jo + Holly ~ How to Add More Depth to Your Marketing
- 203 Jo + Holly ~ How to Find New Ways of Marketing Business Online
- 179 Holly Worton ~ How to Balance Inner Work & Marketing Your Business
- 172 Elizabeth Goddard ~ How to Revolutionize Your Email Marketing With ConvertKit
- 124 Beth Grant ~ How to Align Your Marketing With Who You Are
- 106 Nicci Bonfanti ~ How to Serve Your Clients Through Selling
- 102 Halley Grey ~ How to Create Sales Pages That Work
- 50 How to Plan a Digital Marketing Strategy, with Julia Lera
- 38 How to Get More Clients Saying Yes, with Catherine Watkin

Money

- 278 Joanna Hennon + Holly ~ Success: It's More Than Just Money
- 248 Holly + Joanna Hennon ~ How to Make Money Manifesting Work for You
- 221 Holly Worton ~ How Your Money Mindset Relates to Your Business Mindset
- 170 Denise Duffield-Thomas ~ How Upgrading Your Money Mindset Can Transform Your Business
- 101 Ann Wilson ~ How to Make Your Money Work Hard For You
- 90 How to Overcome Your Money Blocks, with Denise Duffield-Thomas
- 66 How to Heal Your Money Blocks, with Yiye Zhang
- 29 How to Heal Your Money "Stuff" & Find Your Life Purpose, with Mary Jane Allen
- 18 How to Make More Money in Your Business, with Roxy Ahmed

Personal Power

- 297 Holly Worton ~ Personal Power: Why You Need It & How to Get It
- 158 Joanna Hennon ~ Get Better Results in Business by Accessing Your Soul Power
- 120 Amber Lilyestrom ~ How to Step Into Your Power Through Your Brand
- 41 How to Step Into Your Personal Power in Business, with Jac McNeil
- 9 How to Achieve Holistic Self-Empowerment, with Sofia Barao

Strategy, Clarity, and Vision

- 195 Holly Worton ~ How to Stay Grounded + Strong in Your Vision
- 111 Holly Worton ~ How to Get Clear on Your Big Business Vision
- 50 How to Plan a Digital Marketing Strategy, with Julia Lera

Success and Opportunity

- 278 Joanna Hennon + Holly ~ Success: It's More Than Just Money
- 206 Holly Worton ~ Why You've Got to Be 100% Committed to Your Business Success
- 187 Maggie Patterson ~ How to Build A Successful Business From Referrals
- 134 Linda Ursin ~ How to Tap Into Your Female Strengths For Business Success
- 107 Annie Stoker ~ How to Have Stress Free Success in Business & Life
- 33 How to Tap Into Your Success, with Linda Anderson
- 27 How to Build a Successful Business Around Your Blog, with Celestine Chua
- 24 How to Use Your Dreams for Business Success, with Tia Johnson
- 20 How to Build a Successful Coaching Practice, with Sonia Gill

Value and Self-Worth

77 How to Charge What You're Worth & Get It, with Siobhan McAuley Visibility

- 215 Holly Worton ~ Boost Your Visibility With Reviews, Testimonials, Referrals, & Shoutouts
- 213 Holly Worton ~ How to Face the Shadow Side of Visibility With Confidence
- 211 Holly Worton ~ How to Redefine Visibility & Create Deeper Connections Online
- 157 Holly Worton ~ How to Increase Your Visibility by Transforming Your Mindset
- 137 Holly Worton ~ How to Stop Hiding & Overcome Your Fear of Visibility
- 53 How to Raise Your Visibility, with Jenny Kovacs

Transform your business blocks

- 295 Sharon Lock ~ How to Make Mindset Work a Habit
- 245 Holly Worton ~ How to Spring Clean Your Business + Mindset
- 230 Holly Worton ~ How to Make Mindset Work a Habit
- 276 Holly Worton ~ How to Create Your Own Personal Formula For Mindset Work & Healing

ABOUT THE AUTHOR

Holly Worton is a podcaster and nine times published author. Her latest book, *If Trees Could Talk: Life Lessons from the Wisdom of the Woods*, went straight to the top of 16 Amazon bestseller lists, and she has been featured on BBC Radio Scotland and on prime time national television in the UK – on ITV's This Morning.

She helps people get to know themselves better through connecting with Nature, so they can feel happier and more fulfilled. Holly enjoys spending time outdoors, walking long-distance trails and exploring Britain's sacred sites. She's originally from California and now lives in the Surrey Hills, but has also lived in Spain, Costa Rica, Mexico, Chile, and Argentina. Holly is a member of the Druid order OBOD.

Holly ran her first business for ten years, building it up to become a multi-million-dollar enterprise. When she went into the coaching world she was confident that she had the business and marketing skills she needed to set up a new company. And she did – but she struggled to grow her new venture quickly because she encountered fears, blocks, and limiting beliefs that she didn't even know she had.

She discovered that pushing forward and taking action just wasn't enough. She needed to transform her mindset and release her blocks, as this was the only way to take the *right* actions to move her new business forward. Thus began her journey of intense personal development through deep mindset work, which transformed her existing coaching business into a focus on helping people with their business mindset.

Eventually, she realized that she wanted to devote her time to helping people through her writing, and she let go of her mindset business to focus on her books. Now, Holly continues to write about mindset, long-distance walking, and connecting to Nature.

Podcast

You can find her podcast on Apple Podcasts, or wherever you listen to podcasts. Links to subscribe, as well as the full list of episodes, can be found here: http://www.hollyworton.com/podcast/.

Patreon

You can join her online community where you can receive the benefits of her done-for-you mindset work, and also get discounts on one-to-one sessions, by joining her on Patreon: https://www.patreon.com/hollyworton.

Books

You can find her other books, including her books on nature, walking long-distance trails and business mindset, wherever you purchased this book.

Newsletter

Finally, you can stay in touch by subscribing to her newsletter on her main website: http://www.hollyworton.com/.

ALSO BY HOLLY WORTON

Business books

- *Business Beliefs: Upgrade Your Mindset to Overcome Self Sabotage, Achieve Your Goals, and Transform Your Business (and Life)*
- *Business Blocks: Transform Your Self-Sabotaging Mind Gremlins, Awaken Your Inner Mentor, and Allow Your Business Brilliance to Shine*
- *Business Blocks: A Companion Workbook*
- *Business Intuition: Tools to Help You Trust Your Own Instincts, Connect with Your Inner Compass, and Easily Make the Right Decisions*
- *Business Intuition: A Companion Workbook*
- *Business Visibility: Mindset Shifts to Help You Stop Playing Small, Dimming Your Light and Devaluing Your Magic*
- *Business Visibility: A Companion Workbook*

Nature books

- *If Trees Could Talk: Life Lessons from the Wisdom of the Woods*
- *If Trees Could Talk: Life Lessons from the Wisdom of the Woods — A Companion Workbook*

Walking books

- *Alone on the South Downs Way: One Woman's Solo Journey from Winchester to Eastbourne*
- *Walking the Downs Link: Planning Guide & Reflections on Walking from St.*

Martha's Hill to Shoreham-by-Sea

- *Alone on the Ridgeway: One Woman's Solo Journey from Avebury to Ivinghoe Beacon*
- *Walking the Wey-South Path: Planning Guide & Reflections on Walking from Guildford to Amberley*

A Request

If you enjoyed this book, please review it online. It takes just a couple of minutes to write a quick review. It would mean the world to me! Good reviews help other readers to discover new books.

Thank you, thank you, thank you.

Made in the USA
Monee, IL
11 May 2020

30126051R00095